John's Gospel is like a pool in which a lamb may wade and an elephant may swim

Explaining this presentation of John – the layout & illustrations

John works at many levels, with layers of meanings and symbols, which overlay each other to form patterns that comprise its form. It is impossible for me to do justice – or even refer – to all of these. And so I have selected some that I could visualise, hoping that readers use my model to study others.

My illustrations emphasise *John's* themes of light and life reflected in the impact of water in the semi-arid regions of outback Australia. The specimen drawings reflect *John's* allusions to the Creation stories 'In the beginning' and the Garden of Eden, which suggest that Jesus' coming brings about a new and restored Creation. The birds and trees in and beside the water reflect the abundant life that comes from continuing to trust God, which the Gospel calls 'abiding' – that is, remaining or residing – in him. Titles of the paintings link their subjects to those of the text. I pray that their conversation with the text assists your meditation of this wonderful Gospel.

The colouring of the text is to highlight the patterns of courtroom scenes and the blessings Jesus offers.

A few more comments are found in the *Postscript* following the Gospel.

The quip on the previous page is my paraphrase of the quote below, which Naselli traces to Gregory the Great (6th century), quoted and adapted by many commentators on *John*, including Moloney (2005, 5) – with good reason –

> Scripture is like a river again, broad and deep, shallow enough here for the lamb to go wading, but deep enough there for the elephant to swim.
> (Naselli 2009).

Contents of the Gospel

Explaining my presentation of John – the text

I have 'tinkered' with the format of the text to aid understanding.

Overall:

Although the text is presented by discrete units on each page to help the reader understand how I think it fits together, chapter and verse references are missing so that the story flows into one continuous whole

Text is in red-brown, except for blue text discussing the benefits for believers and black for passages that John sets out as episodes in a courtroom drama (see later under Hints for reading John)

Where Jesus (or the writer) speaks in metaphors, or what they call 'figures of speech', the words are centred in poetic form

Truly, truly and ***I am*** statements are frequently in bold italics and centred for emphasis

Where *you* is in italics, it denotes its plural form, where that enhances meaning. Bear in mind that it is so frequently throughout (especially in chapters 13-16) although I have not italicised it

'The Jews' is mostly in quotation marks as a reminder that the term has several meanings or connotations, and the reader needs to consider in which way it is being used in each context (see below)

In chapter 7 italics are used to emphasise the different groups (who act as characters in the story) debating Jesus' identity

In chapters 13-17 I have highlighted words that describe God, including love, joy, and peace – attributes that the Spirit gives those who trust him

In Jesus' prayer in chapter 17, direct requests are in italics

I have substituted contemporary standards for the measurements [in brackets] on pages 7, 39 and 58 so that readers immediately grasp their size

I have also 'tinkered' with the ESV translation of some words.

Firstly, where a Greek word has two possible meanings, the writer means both. So the first time it appears in the references below, I show both, and you should bear the double meaning in mind throughout the remainder of the book. For example:

1. 'grasped' on page 2 (1:5) both (literally) to hold/overcome, and (metaphorically) to understand
2. believe/ entrust on page 8 (2:23-4)
3. born from above/anew on page 8 (3:3)
4. wind/spirit on page 9 (3:5-8)
5. condemn/judge on page 10 (3:17)
6. persecute/prosecute on page 18 (5:16) 'to bring a charge against' (Moloney 1996:8,10)
7. abide/remain page on 29 (8:31, 35)
8. recover/be saved on page 35 (11:12)
9. 'greatly troubled' on page 36 (11:33) encompasses anger and outrage (Carson 1991:415-6), frustration and disappointment (Moloney 1996:169) at death and unbelief
10. 'place' is used on page 38 (11:48) to refer to the Temple – the *symbol* of the meeting place of God with his people – which Jesus calls 'My Father's house' on page 7 (2:16) and which on page 46 (14:2) he means *in reality*, and which has many dwelling places (Dumbrell 2006:141)
11. 'Paraclete' (page 47) is literally one 'called alongside'. It encompasses legal counsel/advocate, one who strengthens, encourages and aids (Carson (1991:499)

Secondly, after consulting commentaries, in places I have altered some words that I feel better reflect their meaning:

a. Page 1 (1:4) 'men' to 'humanity' (Greek *anthropos*)

b. Page 9 (3:5) 'the Spirit' changed to 'spirit' (Carson 1991:195)

c. Page 10 is changed from 'believes in him may have eternal life' to 'believes may have eternal life in him' (Carson 1991:202)

d. Page 14 (4:26) 'I who speak to you am he' changed to 'I am, the one...' to highlight the first of the *I am* sayings. This term is significant in *John*, as it echoes words in the Hebrew Scriptures that refer to the Lord God (especially in Isaiah 40-55, and in particular 41:4 and 43:13). Similar changes are made on page 21 (6:20), page 28 (8:18,24,28), page 44 (13:19), and page 54 (18:5,6,8)

e. Page 42 I have deleted 'who were' between 'his own... in the world' to suggest that Jesus directs his love to *all* believers, both present with him then and throughout history (Dumbrell 2006:135)

f. Page 46 (14:2) 'house' is changed to 'home', the same word as on page 47 (14:23) meaning dwelling place (Carson 1991:489)

g. Page 46 (14:2) 'rooms' is changed to 'abiding places'

h. Page 50 (16:13) 'into' all the truth to 'in' (Carson 1991:539)

i. Page 58 (19:28-9) 'accomplished/fulfilled/completed' has replaced 'finished' (Carson 1991:621) that is, 'brought to perfection' (Moloney 2005:108) – a triumphant shout that the work he was sent into the world to accomplish is completed, not a sigh of defeat

j. Page 58 (19:30) 'gave up' to 'handed over' (Carson 1991:621; and including 'deliver/entrust' (Moloney 1998:146) – ie to the Father – see Luke 23:46

k. Page 62 'glad' to 'overjoyed' (Carson 1991: 647)

References in the manuscript

Carson, DA 1991 *The Gospel According to John* Eerdmans: Grand Rapids

Carter, Warren 2006 *John: Storyteller, Interpreter, Evangelist* Peabody: Hendrickson

Dumbrell, William 2006 *John: Gospel of the New Creation A New Covenant Exposition* Caringbah NSW: New Covenant Publications

Moloney, Francis

　　1996 *Signs and Shadows: Reading John 5-12* Minneapolis: Fortress

　　1998 *Glory not Dishonour: Reading John 13-21* Minneapolis: Augsburg Fortress

　　2005 *The Gospel of John: Text and Context* Boston: Brill Academic

Naselli, Andy 2009 *On Swimming Elephants* http://andynaselli.com/on-swimming-elephants, found 2/9/2013

Painter, John 1991 *The Quest for the Messiah: the history, literature and theology of the Johannine community* Edinburgh: T&T Clark

Stibbe, Mark WG 1994 *John's Gospel* London: Routledge

Recommended reading

For a straightforward, historical study of *John*, I recommend Paul Barnett 2005 *John: The Shepherd King* Sydney: Aquila Press

For a clear, literary approach, see Mark Stibbe's commentary referenced above

Helpful background from the Hebrew Scriptures

Genesis 1-2 – two Creation stories

Psalm 103, particularly vv8-14: God loves, judges justly, and forgives (cf Exodus 34:6-7)

Lamb of God Genesis 22; Exodus 12; Isaiah 53

The story of deliverance from Egypt under Moses' leadership: Exodus 13:17–17:7; 19:1-6 – manna and water, guidance, protection and grumbling; Numbers 21:4-9 – the bronze serpent

The Jewish feasts: Leviticus 23 (apart from the nonbiblical Feast of Dedication that commemorates the Temple's rededication after Hellenist defilement about 2 centuries earlier)

Isaiah 42:1-9; 55:1-3; 65:17-25 – God's chosen one, water, and a new creation

Ezekiel 34, 37 and 47:1-12 – life, shepherds, and water

For me, the Gospel as a whole evokes Moses' farewell speech to Israel on the brink of the Promised Land: 'I call heaven and earth to witness to you today, that I have set before you life and death, blessing and curse. Therefore choose life...' (Deuteronomy 30:19)

Explaining some terms used in the book:

'The Jews' can simply mean people *at the time of the events* who are Jewish (including Jesus, John, and their disciples), also known as Israelites (descended from Israel, formerly called Jacob, grandson of Abraham, to whom in Genesis 12 God made promises that would bless the world). Their country is thus called Israel. Its northern region includes Galilee, and its southern (including Jerusalem) is called Judea, whose inhabitants are called Judeans – or often simply 'Jews'.

But in most cases in *John* 'the Jews' refers to a group that function as one character or role *in John's account of the events*, representing Jesus' opponents, whose attitude is of fixed and wilful resistance to him (eg p18-19), or who turn back from following him (p29). This group includes some of the priests (appointed to serve in the Temple) and Pharisees (who thought they could achieve 'perfection' in God's sight by meticulously keeping his law given through Moses, and imposed on others to do likewise). They wielded enormous social power, but the nation was under Roman subjection, under its governor Pilate.

Samaria was a separate region to the northwest, settled by non-Jews, who traced their heritage to Jacob centuries earlier. The two peoples were not on good terms, the Jews despising the Samaritans.

'The Christ' is Greek for the Hebrew 'Messiah', God's unique Anointed One. In the Hebrew Scriptures (the Christian Old Testament), high priests, kings and sometimes prophets were anointed, but this one is something far more than the sum of these parts.

'The Son of Man' can simply mean human, but it is also a specific title coming from Daniel 7, where God gives 'one like a son of man' authority forever over all humanity.

A denarius is a day's wages for a labourer, see page 20 (6:7) and 39 (12:5)

Hints for reading John

John was written to be read as a whole, and not piecemeal. Read it right through first. It is like a snowball, building up meaning as it progresses. The Prologue sets the cosmic context and the agenda that the rest of the book addresses. Like Jesus' garment for which soldiers under his cross gambled, *John* is seamless. As you study parts – either episodes or themes – consider them in the light of the Prologue, and integrate them into the whole. At the end of your study series, again read the whole of *John*.

You could study themes running throughout the whole or a part (see my description of the bigger units earlier), such as:

- What aspects of Jesus' character do you see from his words and actions? (eg his *I am* and *Truly, truly* sayings; his signs; his interactions with people)

- *God: Father, Son and Spirit*

- *The hour*

- The benefits of trusting/believing/receiving/abiding in Jesus, and the consequences of unbelief, including Life and death; Light and dark, day and night; and more...

- Glory and *lifted up*

- The courtroom drama: 'the Jews' v Jesus and his defence; Jesus as God's representative v 'the Jews', leading to the judgement and sentencing by Pilate

- Truth and lies

- Pairs (contrasting or complementing): characters, incidents, ideas

- Sets of sevens (in the Hebrew mindset 7 denotes complete or whole): put together like puzzle pieces into a whole picture

- Words associated with the Spirit, particularly in chapters 13-17

- Like Carter, Painter and Stibbe, look at the elements of John's plot:
  - Individual themes in the Prologue fleshed out in the story
  - Symbols
  - The interplay of action and dialogue; literal and metaphorical
  - Geography
  - Festivals and other Jewish customs
  - Individual characters and their development
  - Who is seeking what?
  - Contrasts

The Gospel
according to
John
illuminated

In the English Standard Version of the Bible *with illustrations of the Australian outback by* Fiona Pfennigwerth

In the beginning was the Word,
      and the Word was with God,
      and the Word was God.
          He was in the beginning with God.
All things were made through him,
      and without him was not any thing made that was made.

In him was life
and the life was the light of humanity[a].
      The light shines in the darkness,
          and the darkness has not grasped[1] it.

There was a man sent from God, whose name was John.
      He came as a witness, to bear witness about the light, that all might believe through him.
      He was not the light, but came to bear witness about the light.

      The true light, which enlightens everyone, was coming into the world.
          He was in the world,
          and the world was made through him,
          yet the world did not know him.
          He came to his own,
          and his own people did not receive him.

But to all who did receive him,
who believed in his name,
he gave the right to become children of God,
who were born, not of blood nor of the will of the flesh
nor of the will of man,
but of God.

And the Word became flesh and dwelt among us,

and we have seen his glory,

glory as of the only Son from the Father,
full of grace and truth.

(John bore witness about him, and cried out,
"This was he of whom I said,
'He who comes after me ranks before me, because he was before me.'")

And from his fullness we have all received, grace upon grace.
For the law was given through Moses;
grace and truth came through Jesus Christ.
No one has ever seen God;
the only God, who is at the Father's side,
he has made him known.

And this is the testimony of John,

when 'the Jews' sent priests and Levites from Jerusalem to ask him, "Who are you?" He confessed, and did not deny, but confessed, "I am not the Christ." And they asked him, "What then? Are you Elijah?" He said, "I am not." "Are you the Prophet?" And he answered, "No." So they said to him, "Who are you? We need to give an answer to those who sent us. What do you say about yourself?" He said,

"I am the voice of one crying out in the wilderness,
'Make straight the way of the Lord,' as the prophet Isaiah said."

(Now they had been sent from the Pharisees.) They asked him, "Then why are you baptizing, if you are neither the Christ, nor Elijah, nor the Prophet?" John answered them, "I baptize with water, but among you stands one you do not know, even he who comes after me, the strap of whose sandal I am not worthy to untie." These things took place in Bethany across the Jordan, where John was baptizing.

The next day he saw Jesus coming toward him, and said,

"Behold, the Lamb of God, who takes away the sin of the world!
This is he of whom I said, 'After me comes a man who ranks before me, because he was before me.' I myself did not know him, but for this purpose I came baptizing with water, that he might be revealed to Israel."

And John bore witness: "I saw the Spirit descend from heaven like a dove, and it remained on him. I myself did not know him, but he who sent me to baptize with water said to me, 'He on whom you see the Spirit descend and remain, this is he who baptizes with the Holy Spirit.' And I have seen and have borne witness that this is the Son of God."

The next day again John was standing with two of his disciples, and he looked at Jesus as he walked by and said,

"Behold, the Lamb of God!"

The two disciples heard him say this, and they followed Jesus.

Jesus turned and saw them following and said to them,

"What are you seeking?"

And they said to him, "Rabbi" (which means Teacher), "where are you staying?" He said to them,
"Come and you will see."

So they came and saw where he was staying, and they stayed with him that day, for it was about the tenth hour.

One of the two who heard John speak and followed Jesus was Andrew, Simon Peter's brother. He first found his own brother Simon and said to him, "We have found the Messiah" (which means Christ). He brought him to Jesus. Jesus looked at him and said, "So you are Simon the son of John? You shall be called Cephas" (which means Peter).

The next day Jesus decided to go to Galilee. He found Philip and said to him, "Follow me." Now Philip was from Bethsaida, the city of Andrew and Peter. Philip found Nathanael and said to him, "We have found him of whom Moses in the Law and also the prophets wrote, Jesus of Nazareth, the son of Joseph." Nathanael said to him, "Can anything good come out of Nazareth?" Philip said to him,
"Come and see."

Jesus saw Nathanael coming toward him and said of him, "Behold, an Israelite indeed, in whom there is no deceit!" Nathanael said to him, "How do you know me?" Jesus answered him, "Before Philip called you, when you were under the fig tree, I saw you." Nathanael answered him, "Rabbi, you are the Son of God! You are the King of Israel!" Jesus answered him, "Because I said to you, 'I saw you under the fig tree,' do you believe? You will see greater things than these." And he said to him,
"Truly, truly, I say to you,
you will see heaven opened,
and the angels of God ascending and descending on the Son of Man."

On the third day there was a wedding at Cana in Galilee, and the mother of Jesus was there. Jesus also was invited to the wedding with his disciples. When the wine ran out, the mother of Jesus said to him, "They have no wine." And Jesus said to her, "Woman, what does this have to do with me? My hour has not yet come." His mother said to the servants, "Do whatever he tells you." Now there were six stone water jars there for the Jewish rites of purification, each holding about [thirty five litres]. Jesus said to the servants, "Fill the jars with water." And they filled them up to the brim. And he said to them, "Now draw some out and take it to the master of the feast." So they took it. When the master of the feast tasted the water now become wine, and did not know where it came from (though the servants who had drawn the water knew), the master of the feast called the bridegroom and said to him, "Everyone serves the good wine first, and when people have drunk freely, then the poor wine. But you have kept the good wine until now." This, the first of his signs, Jesus did at Cana in Galilee, and manifested his glory. And his disciples believed in him.

After this he went down to Capernaum, with his mother and his brothers and his disciples, and they stayed there for a few days.

In the temple he found those who were selling oxen and sheep and pigeons, and the money-changers sitting there. And making a whip of cords, he drove them all out of the temple, with the sheep and oxen. And he poured out the coins of the money-changers and overturned their tables. And he told those who sold the pigeons, "Take these things away; do not make my Father's house a house of trade." His disciples remembered that it was written, "Zeal for your house will consume me."

So 'the Jews' said to him, "What sign do you show us for doing these things?" Jesus answered them, "Destroy this temple, and in three days I will raise it up." 'The Jews' then said, "It has taken forty-six years to build this temple, and will you raise it up in three days?" But he was speaking about the temple of his body. When therefore he was raised from the dead, his disciples remembered that he had said this, and they believed the Scripture and the word that Jesus had spoken.

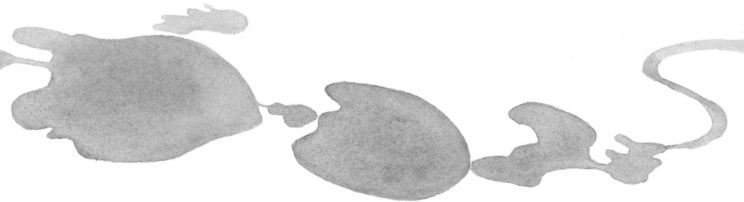

John 2:1-22

Now when he was in Jerusalem

at the Passover Feast,

many believed/trusted[2] in his name when they saw the signs that he was doing. But Jesus on his part did not entrust[2] himself to them, because he knew all people and needed no one to bear witness about man, for he himself knew what was in man. Now there was a man of the Pharisees named Nicodemus, a ruler of 'the Jews'. This man came to Jesus by night and said to him, "Rabbi, we know that you are a teacher come from God, for no one can do these signs that you do unless God is with him."

Jesus answered him,
"Truly, truly, I say to you,
unless one is born from above/again[3] he cannot see the kingdom of God."

John 2:23-3:3

Nicodemus said to him, "How can a man be born when he is old? Can he enter a second time into his mother's womb and be born?" Jesus answered,

"Truly, truly, I say to you, unless one is born of water and spirit[6], he cannot enter the kingdom of God.

"That which is born of the flesh is flesh, and that which is born of the Spirit is spirit. Do not marvel that I said to you, 'You must be born again.' The wind/spirit[4] blows where it wishes, and you hear its sound, but you do not know where it comes from or where it goes. So it is with everyone who is born of the Spirit.

Nicodemus said to him, "How can these things be?" Jesus answered him,
"Are you the teacher of Israel and yet you do not understand these things?
Truly, truly, I say to you,
we speak of what we know, and bear witness to what we have seen,
but *you* do not receive our testimony.
If I have told *you* earthly things and *you* do not believe,
how can *you* believe if I tell *you* heavenly things?
No one has ascended into heaven except he who descended from heaven,
the Son of Man.
And as Moses lifted up the serpent in the wilderness,
so must the Son of Man be lifted up,
that whoever believes may have eternal life in him[c].

For God so loved the world,

that he gave his only Son,

that whoever believes in him should not perish

but have eternal life.

For God did not send his Son into the world to condemn/judge[5] the world,
but in order that the world might be saved through him.
Whoever believes in him is not condemned,
but whoever does not believe is condemned already,
because he has not believed in the name of the only Son of God.
And this is the judgment: the light has come into the world,
and people loved the darkness rather than the light
because their works were evil.
For everyone who does wicked things hates the light
and does not come to the light, lest his works should be exposed.
But whoever does what is true comes to the light,
so that it may be clearly seen that his works have been carried out in God.

John 3:9-21

After this Jesus and his disciples went into the Judean countryside, and he remained there with them and was baptizing. John also was baptizing at Aenon near Salim, because water was plentiful there, and people were coming and being baptized (for John had not yet been put in prison).

Now a discussion arose between some of John's disciples and a 'Jew' over purification. And they came to John and said to him, "Rabbi, he who was with you across the Jordan, to whom you bore witness—look, he is baptizing, and all are going to him." John answered, "A person cannot receive even one thing unless it is given him from heaven. You yourselves bear me witness, that I said, 'I am not the Christ, but I have been sent before him.' The one who has the bride is the bridegroom. The friend of the bridegroom, who stands and hears him, rejoices greatly at the bridegroom's voice. Therefore this joy of mine is now complete. He must increase, but I must decrease.

He who comes from above is above all.
He who is of the earth belongs to the earth and speaks in an earthly way.
He who comes from heaven is above all.
He bears witness to what he has seen and heard,
yet no one receives his testimony.
Whoever receives his testimony sets his seal to this, that God is true.

For he whom God has sent utters the words of God,

for he gives the Spirit without measure.

The Father loves the Son

and has given all things into his hand.

Whoever believes in the Son has eternal life;

whoever does not obey the Son shall not see life,
but the wrath of God remains on him.

Now

when Jesus learned that the Pharisees had heard that Jesus was making and baptizing more disciples than John (although Jesus himself did not baptize, but only his disciples), he left Judea and departed again for Galilee. And he had to pass through Samaria.

So he came to a town of Samaria called Sychar, near the field that Jacob had given to his son Joseph. Jacob's well was there; so Jesus, wearied as he was from his journey, was sitting beside the well. It was about the sixth hour.

A woman from Samaria came to draw water. Jesus said to her, "Give me a drink." (For his disciples had gone away into the city to buy food.) The Samaritan woman said to him, "How is it that you, a Jew, ask for a drink from me, a woman of Samaria?" For Jews have no dealings with Samaritans.) Jesus answered her,

"If you knew the gift of God,
and who it is that is saying to you, 'Give me a drink,'
you would have asked him, and he would have given you living water."

The woman said to him, "Sir, you have nothing to draw water with, and the well is deep. Where do you get that living water? Are you greater than our father Jacob? He gave us the well and drank from it himself, as did his sons and his livestock."

Jesus said to her, "Everyone who drinks of this water will be thirsty again,
but whoever drinks of the water that I will give him
will never be thirsty forever.

John 4:1-14a

"The water that I will give him will become in him
a spring of water welling up to eternal life."

The woman said to him, "Sir, give me this water, so that I will not be thirsty or have to come here to draw water."

Jesus said to her, "Go, call your husband, and come here." The woman answered him, "I have no husband." Jesus said to her, "You are right in saying, 'I have no husband'; for you have had five husbands, and the one you now have is not your husband. What you have said is true." The woman said to him, "Sir, I perceive that you are a prophet. Our fathers worshiped on this mountain, but you say that in Jerusalem is the place where people ought to worship." Jesus said to her, "Woman, believe me, the hour is coming when neither on this mountain nor in Jerusalem will you worship the Father. You worship what you do not know; we worship what we know, for salvation is from 'the Jews'.

But the hour is coming, and is now here,

when the true worshipers will worship the Father

in spirit and truth,

for the Father is seeking such people to worship him.
God is spirit,
and those who worship him must worship in spirit and truth."

The woman said to him, "I know that Messiah is coming (he who is called Christ). When he comes, he will tell us all things."

Jesus said to her, **"I am, the one who speaks to you."**[d]

Just then his disciples came back. They marvelled that he was talking with a woman, but no one said, "What do you seek?" or, "Why are you talking with her?" So the woman left her water jar and went away into town and said to the people, "Come, see a man who told me all that I ever did. Can this be the Christ?" They went out of the town and were coming to him. Meanwhile the disciples were urging him, saying, "Rabbi, eat." But he said to them, "I have food to eat that you do not know about." So the disciples said to one another, "Has anyone brought him something to eat?" Jesus said to them, "My food is to do the will of him who sent me and to accomplish his work. Do you not say, 'There are yet four months, then comes the harvest'? Look, I tell you, lift up your eyes, and see that the fields are white for harvest. Already the one who reaps is receiving wages and gathering fruit for eternal life, so that sower and reaper may rejoice together. For here the saying holds true, 'One sows and another reaps.' I sent you to reap that for which you did not labour. Others have laboured, and you have entered into their labour."

Many Samaritans from that town believed in him because of the woman's testimony, "He told me all that I ever did." So when the Samaritans came to him, they asked him to stay with them, and he stayed there two days. And many more believed because of his word. They said to the woman, "It is no longer because of what you said that we believe, for we have heard for ourselves, and we know that this is indeed the Saviour of the world."

After the two days he departed for Galilee. (For Jesus himself had testified that a prophet has no honour in his own hometown.) So when he came to Galilee, the Galileans welcomed him, having seen all that he had done in Jerusalem at the feast. For they too had gone to the feast.

So he came again to Cana in Galilee, where he had made the water wine. And at Capernaum there was an official whose son was ill. When this man heard that Jesus had come from Judea to Galilee, he went to him and asked him to come down and heal his son, for he was at the point of death. So Jesus said to him, "Unless *you* see signs and wonders *you* will not believe." The official said to him, "Sir, come down before my child dies." Jesus said to him, "Go; your son will live."

The man believed the word that Jesus spoke to him and went on his way.

As he was going down, his servants met him and told him that his son was recovering. So he asked them the hour when he began to get better, and they said to him, "Yesterday at the seventh hour the fever left him." The father knew that was the hour when Jesus had said to him, "Your son will live." And he himself believed, and all his household.

This was now the second sign that Jesus did when he had come from Judea to Galilee.

After this there was a feast of the Jews,
and Jesus went up to Jerusalem.

Now there is in Jerusalem by the Sheep Gate a pool, in Aramaic called Bethesda, which has five roofed colonnades. In these lay a multitude of invalids—blind, lame, and paralysed. One man was there who had been an invalid for thirty-eight years. When Jesus saw him lying there and knew that he had already been there a long time, he said to him, "Do you want to be healed?" The sick man answered him, "Sir, I have no one to put me into the pool when the water is stirred up, and while I am going another steps down before me." Jesus said to him, "Get up, take up your bed, and walk." And at once the man was healed, and he took up his bed and walked.

Now that day was the Sabbath. So 'the Jews' said to the man who had been healed, "It is the Sabbath, and it is not lawful for you to take up your bed." But he answered them, "The man who healed me, that man said to me, 'Take up your bed, and walk.'" They asked him, "Who is the man who said to you, 'Take up your bed and walk'?" Now the man who had been healed did not know who it was, for Jesus had withdrawn, as there was a crowd in the place. Afterward Jesus found him in the temple and said to him, "See, you are well! Sin no more, that nothing worse may happen to you." The man went away and told 'the Jews' that it was Jesus who had healed him.

And this was why 'the Jews' were persecuting/prosecuting[6] Jesus, because he was doing these things on the Sabbath. But Jesus answered them,

"My Father is working until now, and I am working."

This was why 'the Jews' were seeking all the more to kill him, because not only was he breaking the Sabbath, but he was even calling God his own Father, making himself equal with God. So Jesus said to them,

"Truly, truly, I say to you,
the Son can do nothing of his own accord,
but only what he sees the Father doing.
For whatever the Father does, that the Son does likewise.
For the Father loves the Son and shows him all that he himself is doing. And greater works than these will he show him, so that you may marvel.
For as the Father raises the dead and gives them life,
so also the Son gives life to whom he will.
The Father judges no one, but has given all judgment to the Son, that all may honour the Son, just as they honour the Father. Whoever does not honour the Son does not honour the Father who sent him.
Truly, truly, I say to you,
whoever hears my word and believes him who sent me has eternal life.
He does not come into judgment, but has passed from death to life.
Truly, truly, I say to you,
an hour is coming, and is now here,
when the dead will hear the voice of the Son of God,
and those who hear will live.
For as the Father has life in himself, so he has granted the Son also to have life in himself. And he has given him authority to execute judgment, because he is the Son of Man.

"Do not marvel at this, for an hour is coming when all who are in the tombs will hear his voice and come out, those who have done good to the resurrection of life, and those who have done evil to the resurrection of judgment.
I can do nothing on my own.
As I hear, I judge, and my judgment is just,
because I seek not my own will but the will of him who sent me."

John 5:16-30

"If I alone bear witness about myself, my testimony is not deemed true. There is another who bears witness about me, and I know that the testimony that he bears about me is true.

- You sent to John, and he has borne witness to the truth. Not that the testimony that I receive is from man, but I say these things so that you may be saved. He was a burning and shining lamp, and you were willing to rejoice for a while in his light. But the testimony that I have is greater than that of John.

- For the works that the Father has given me to accomplish, the very works that I am doing, bear witness about me that the Father has sent me. And the Father who sent me has himself borne witness about me. His voice you have never heard, his form you have never seen, and you do not have his word abiding in you, for you do not believe the one whom he has sent.

- You search the Scriptures because you think that in them you have eternal life; and it is they that bear witness about me, yet you refuse to come to me that you may have life.

"I do not receive glory from people. But I know that you do not have the love of God within you. I have come in my Father's name, and you do not receive me. If another comes in his own name, you will receive him. How can you believe, when you receive glory from one another and do not seek the glory that comes from the only God?

- Do not think that I will accuse you to the Father. There is one who accuses you: Moses, on whom you have set your hope. For if you believed Moses, you would believe me; for he wrote of me. But if you do not believe his writings, how will you believe my words?"

After this Jesus went away to the other side of the Sea of Galilee, which is the Sea of Tiberias. And a large crowd was following him, because they saw the signs that he was doing on the sick. Jesus went up on the mountain, and there he sat down with his disciples.

*Now the Passover, the feast of the Jews,
was at hand.*

Lifting up his eyes, then, and seeing that a large crowd was coming toward him, Jesus said to Philip, "Where are we to buy bread, so that these people may eat?" He said this to test him, for he himself knew what he would do.

Philip answered him, "Two hundred denarii would not buy enough bread for each of them to get a little." One of his disciples, Andrew, Simon Peter's brother, said to him, "There is a boy here who has five barley loaves and two fish, but what are they for so many?" Jesus said, "Have the people sit down."

Now there was much grass in the place. So the men sat down, about five thousand in number. Jesus then took the loaves, and when he had given thanks, he distributed them to those who were seated. So also the fish, as much as they wanted.

And when they had eaten their fill, he told his disciples, "Gather up the leftover fragments, *that nothing may be lost.*" So they gathered them up and filled twelve baskets with fragments from the five barley loaves left by those who had eaten.

When the people saw the sign that he had done, they said, "This is indeed the Prophet who is to come into the world!"

Perceiving then that they were about to come and take him by force to make him king, Jesus withdrew again to the mountain by himself.

When evening came, his disciples went down to the sea, got into a boat, and started across the sea to Capernaum. It was now dark, and Jesus had not yet come to them. The sea became rough because a strong wind was blowing. When they had rowed about three or four miles, they saw Jesus walking on the sea and coming near the boat, and they were frightened. But he said to them,

"I am; do not be afraid."

Then they were glad to take him into the boat, and immediately the boat was at the land to which they were going.

On the next day the crowd that remained on the other side of the sea saw that there had been only one boat there, and that Jesus had not entered the boat with his disciples, but that his disciples had gone away alone. Other boats from Tiberias came near the place where they had eaten the bread after the Lord had given thanks. So when the crowd saw that Jesus was not there, nor his disciples, they themselves got into the boats and went to Capernaum, seeking Jesus. When they found him on the other side of the sea, they said to him, "Rabbi, when did you come here?"

Jesus answered them, *"Truly, truly, I say to you*, you are seeking me, not because you saw signs, but because you ate your fill of the loaves.
Do not labour for the food that perishes,
but for the food that endures to eternal life,
which the Son of Man will give to you.
For on him God the Father has set his seal."

Then they said to him, "What must we do, to be doing the works of God?" Jesus answered them, "This is the work of God, that you believe in him whom he has sent."

So they said to him, "Then what sign do you do, that we may see and believe you? What work do you perform? Our fathers ate the manna in the wilderness; as it is written, 'He gave them bread from heaven to eat.'" Jesus then said to them,
"Truly, truly, I say to you,
it was not Moses who gave you the bread from heaven,
but my Father gives you the true bread from heaven.

For the bread of God is he who comes down from heaven
and gives life to the world."

They said to him, "Sir, give us this bread always."

Jesus said to them,

"I am the bread of life;
whoever comes to me shall not hunger,
and whoever believes in me shall never thirst.
But I said to you that you have seen me and yet do not believe.
All that the Father gives me will come to me,
and whoever comes to me I will never cast out.
For I have come down from heaven,
not to do my own will but the will of him who sent me.
And this is the will of him who sent me,
that I should *lose nothing* of all that he has given me,
but raise it up on the last day.

For this is the will of my Father,
that everyone who looks on the Son and believes in him
should have eternal life,
and I will raise him up on the last day."

So 'the Jews' grumbled about him, because he said, "I am the bread that came down from heaven." They said, "Is not this Jesus, the son of Joseph, whose father and mother we know? How does he now say, 'I have come down from heaven'?"

Jesus answered them, "Do not grumble among yourselves. No one can come to me unless the Father who sent me draws him. And I will raise him up on the last day. It is written in the Prophet,
'And they will all be taught by God.'
Everyone who has heard and learned from the Father comes to me — not that anyone has seen the Father except he who is from God; he has seen the Father.
Truly, truly, I say to you, whoever believes has eternal life.
I am the bread of life.
Your fathers ate the manna in the wilderness, and they died.
This is the bread that comes down from heaven,
so that one may eat of it and not die.

I am the living bread that came down from heaven.
If anyone eats of this bread,
he will live forever.

And the bread that I will give for the life of the world is my flesh."

'The Jews' then disputed among themselves, saying, "How can this man give us his flesh to eat?" So Jesus said to them,
"*Truly, truly, I say to you,*
unless you eat the flesh of the Son of Man and drink his blood,
you have no life in you.
Whoever feeds on my flesh and drinks my blood has eternal life,
and I will raise him up on the last day.
For my flesh is true food, and my blood is true drink.
Whoever feeds on my flesh and drinks my blood abides in me,
and I in him.

As the living Father sent me, and I live because of the Father,
so whoever feeds on me, he also will live because of me.
This is the bread that came down from heaven,
not like the bread the fathers ate and died.
Whoever feeds on this bread will live forever."

Jesus said these things in the synagogue, as he taught at Capernaum.

When many of his disciples heard it, they said, "This is a hard saying; who can listen to it?" But Jesus, knowing in himself that his disciples were grumbling about this, said to them, "Do you take offense at this? Then what if you were to see the Son of Man ascending to where he was before? It is the Spirit who gives life; the flesh is no help at all. The words that I have spoken to you are spirit and life. But there are some of you who do not believe." (For Jesus knew from the beginning who those were who did not believe, and who it was who would betray him.) And he said, "This is why I told you that no one can come to me unless it is granted him by the Father."

After this many of his disciples turned back and no longer walked with him.

So Jesus said to the Twelve, "Do you want to go away as well?"
Simon Peter answered him,
"Lord, to whom shall we go?

You have the words of eternal life,

and we have believed, and have come to know,
that you are the Holy One of God."

Jesus answered them, "Did I not choose you, the Twelve? And yet one of you is a devil." He spoke of Judas the son of Simon Iscariot, for he, one of the Twelve, was going to betray him.

After this Jesus went about in Galilee. He would not go about in Judea, because the Jews were seeking to kill him.

Now the Jews' Feast of Booths was at hand.

So *his brothers* said to him, "Leave here and go to Judea, that your disciples also may see the works you are doing. For no one works in secret if he seeks to be known openly. If you do these things, show yourself to the world." For not even his brothers believed in him. Jesus said to them, "My time has not yet come, but your time is always here. The world cannot hate you, but it hates me because I testify about it that its works are evil. You go up to the feast. I am not going up to this feast, for my time has not yet fully come." After saying this, he remained in Galilee. But after his brothers had gone up to the feast, then he also went up, not publicly but in private.

'The Jews' were looking for him at the feast, and saying, "Where is he?" And there was much muttering about him among *the people*. While some said, "He is a good man," others said, "No, he is leading the people astray." Yet for fear of 'the Jews' no one spoke openly of him.

About the middle of the feast Jesus went up into the temple and began teaching.

'The Jews' therefore marvelled, saying, "How is it that this man has learning, when he has never studied?" So Jesus answered them, "My teaching is not mine, but his who sent me. If anyone's will is to do God's will, he will know whether the teaching is from God or whether I am speaking on my own authority. The one who speaks on his own authority seeks his own glory; but the one who seeks the glory of him who sent him is true, and in him there is no falsehood. Has not Moses given you the law? Yet none of you keeps the law. Why do you seek to kill me?"

The crowd answered, "You have a demon! Who is seeking to kill you?" Jesus answered them, "I did one work, and you all marvel at it. Moses gave you circumcision (not that it is from Moses, but from the fathers), and you circumcise a man on the Sabbath. If on the Sabbath a man receives circumcision, so that the law of Moses may not be broken, are you angry with me because on the Sabbath I made a man's whole body well? Do not judge by appearances, but judge with right judgment."

Some of the people of Jerusalem therefore said, "Is not this the man whom they seek to kill? And here he is, speaking openly, and they say nothing to him! Can it be that the authorities really know that this is the Christ? But we know where this man comes from, and when the Christ appears, no one will know where he comes from." So Jesus proclaimed, as he taught in the temple, "You know me, and you know where I come from? But I have not come of my own accord. He who sent me is true, and him you do not know. I know him, for I come from him, and he sent me." So they were seeking to arrest him, but no one laid a hand on him, because his hour had not yet come. Yet *many of the people* believed in him. They said, "When the Christ appears, will he do more signs than this man has done?"

The Pharisees heard the crowd muttering these things about him, and *the chief priests and Pharisees* sent officers to arrest him. Jesus then said, "I will be with you a little longer, and then I am going to him who sent me. You will seek me and you will not find me. Where I am you cannot come." 'The Jews' said to one another, "Where does this man intend to go that we will not find him? Does he intend to go to the Dispersion among the Greeks and teach the Greeks? What does he mean by saying, 'You will seek me and you will not find me,' and, 'Where I am you cannot come'?"

On the last day of the feast, the great day,
Jesus stood up and cried out,

"If anyone thirsts, let him come to me and drink.

Whoever believes in me,

as the Scripture has said,

'Out of his heart will flow

rivers of living water.'"

Now this he said about the Spirit, whom those who believed in him were to receive, for as yet the Spirit had not been given, because Jesus was not yet glorified.

When they heard these words, *some of the people* said, "This really is the Prophet." *Others* said, "This is the Christ." But *some* said, "Is the Christ to come from Galilee? Has not the Scripture said that the Christ comes from the offspring of David, and comes from Bethlehem, the village where David was?" So there was a division among the people over him.

Some of them wanted to arrest him, but no one laid hands on him.

The officers then came to the chief priests and Pharisees, who said to them, "Why did you not bring him?" The officers answered, "No one ever spoke like this man!" The Pharisees answered them, "Have you also been deceived? Have any of the authorities or the Pharisees believed in him? But this crowd that does not know the law is accursed." Nicodemus, who had gone to him before, and who was one of them, said to them, "Does our law judge a man without first giving him a hearing and learning what he does?" They replied, "Are you from Galilee too? Search and see that no prophet arises from Galilee."

Again Jesus spoke to them, saying,

"I am the light of the world.
Whoever follows me will not walk in darkness,
but will have the light of life."

John 8:12

So *the Pharisees* said to him, "You are bearing witness about yourself; your testimony is not true." Jesus answered, "Even if I do bear witness about myself, my testimony is true, for I know where I came from and where I am going, but you do not know where I come from or where I am going. You judge according to the flesh; I judge no one. Yet even if I do judge, my judgment is true, for it is not I alone who judge, but I and the Father who sent me. In your Law it is written that the testimony of two people is true. *I am* the one who bears witness about myself, and the Father who sent me bears witness about me." They said to him therefore, "Where is your Father?" Jesus answered, "You know neither me nor my Father. If you knew me, you would know my Father also."

These words he spoke in the treasury, as he taught in the temple; but no one arrested him, because his hour had not yet come. So he said to them again, "I am going away, and you will seek me, and you will die in your sin. Where I am going, you cannot come." So 'the Jews' said, "Will he kill himself, since he says, 'Where I am going, you cannot come'?" He said to them,

"You are from below; I am from above.
You are of this world; I am not of this world.
I told you that you would die in your sins,
for unless you believe that *I am* you will die in your sins."

So they said to him, "Who are you?" Jesus said to them, "Just what I have been telling you from the beginning. I have much to say about you and much to judge, but he who sent me is true, and I declare to the world what I have heard from him." They did not understand that he had been speaking to them about the Father. So Jesus said to them,

"When you have lifted up the Son of Man,
then you will know that *I am,*
and that I do nothing on my own authority,
but speak just as the Father taught me."

And he who sent me is with me. He has not left me alone, for I always do the things that are pleasing to him."

As he was saying these things, many believed in him.

So Jesus said to 'the Jews' who had believed in him,

"If you abide in my word, you are truly my disciples,

and you will know the truth,

and the truth will set you free."

They answered him, "We are offspring of Abraham and have never been enslaved to anyone. How is it that you say, 'You will become free'?" Jesus answered them,

"Truly, truly, I say to you,

everyone who commits sin is a slave to sin.

The slave does not remain in the house forever;

the son remains forever.

So if the Son sets you free, you will be free indeed.

I know that you are offspring of Abraham; yet you seek to kill me because my word finds no place in you. I speak of what I have seen with my Father, and you do what you have heard from your father." They answered him, "Abraham is our father." Jesus said to them, "If you were Abraham's children, you would be doing the works Abraham did, but now you seek to kill me, a man who has told you the truth that I heard from God. This is not what Abraham did. You are doing the works your father did."

They said to him, "We were not born of sexual immorality. We have one Father—even God." Jesus said to them, "If God were your Father, you would love me, for I came from God and I am here. I came not of my own accord, but he sent me. Why do you not understand what I say? It is because you cannot bear to hear my word. You are of your father the devil, and your will is to do your father's desires. He was a murderer from the beginning, and has nothing to do with the truth, because there is no truth in him. When he lies, he speaks out of his own character, for he is a liar and the father of lies. But because I tell the truth, you do not believe me. Which one of you convicts me of sin? If I tell the truth, why do you not believe me? Whoever is of God hears the words of God. The reason why you do not hear them is that you are not of God."

'The Jews' answered him, "Are we not right in saying that you are a Samaritan and have a demon?" Jesus answered, "I do not have a demon, but I honour my Father, and you dishonour me. Yet I do not seek my own glory; there is One who seeks it, and he is the judge.

Truly, truly, I say to you,
if anyone keeps my word, he will never see death."

'The Jews' said to him, "Now we know that you have a demon! Abraham died, as did the prophets, yet you say, 'If anyone keeps my word, he will never taste death.' Are you greater than our father Abraham, who died? And the prophets died! Who do you make yourself out to be?" Jesus answered, "If I glorify myself, my glory is nothing. It is my Father who glorifies me, of whom you say, 'He is our God.' But you have not known him. I know him. If I were to say that I do not know him, I would be a liar like you, but I do know him and I keep his word. Your father Abraham rejoiced that he would see my day. He saw it and was glad." So 'the Jews' said to him, "You are not yet fifty years old, and have you seen Abraham?" Jesus said to them,

"Truly, truly, I say to you,
before Abraham was, I am."

So they picked up stones to throw at him, but Jesus hid himself and went out of the temple.

As he passed by, he saw a man blind from birth. And his disciples asked him, "Rabbi, who sinned, this man or his parents, that he was born blind?" Jesus answered, "It was not that this man sinned, or his parents, but that the works of God might be displayed in him. We must work the works of him who sent me while it is day; night is coming, when no one can work.

As long as I am in the world,

I am the light of the world."

Having said these things, he spat on the ground and made mud with the saliva. Then he anointed the man's eyes with the mud and said to him, "Go, wash in the pool of Siloam" (which means Sent). So he went and washed and came back seeing.

The neighbours and those who had seen him before as a beggar were saying, "Is this not the man who used to sit and beg?" Some said, "It is he." Others said, "No, but he is like him." He kept saying, "I am the man." So they said to him, "Then how were your eyes opened?" He answered, "The man called Jesus made mud and anointed my eyes and said to me, 'Go to Siloam and wash.' So I went and washed and received my sight." They said to him, "Where is he?" He said, "I do not know."

They brought to the Pharisees the man who had formerly been blind. Now it was a Sabbath day when Jesus made the mud and opened his eyes. So the Pharisees again asked him how he had received his sight. And he said to them, "He put mud on my eyes, and I washed, and I see." Some of the Pharisees said, "This man is not from God, for he does not keep the Sabbath." But others said, "How can a man who is a sinner do such signs?" And there was a division among them. So they said again to the blind man, "What do you say about him, since he has opened your eyes?" He said, "He is a prophet."

'The Jews' did not believe that he had been blind and had received his sight, until they called the parents of the man who had received his sight and asked them, "Is this your son, who you say was born blind? How then does he now see?" His parents answered, "We know that this is our son and that he was born blind. But how he now sees we do not know, nor do we know who opened his eyes. Ask him; he is of age. He will speak for himself." (His parents said these things because they feared 'the Jews', for 'the Jews' had already agreed that if anyone should confess Jesus to be Christ, he was to be put out of the synagogue.) Therefore his parents said, "He is of age; ask him."

So for the second time they called the man who had been blind and said to him, "Give glory to God. We know that this man is a sinner." He answered, "Whether he is a sinner I do not know. One thing I do know, that though I was blind, now I see."

They said to him, "What did he do to you? How did he open your eyes?" He answered them, "I have told you already, and you would not listen. Why do you want to hear it again? Do you also want to become his disciples?" And they reviled him, saying, "You are his disciple, but we are disciples of Moses. We know that God has spoken to Moses, but as for this man, we do not know where he comes from." The man answered, "Why, this is an amazing thing! You do not know where he comes from, and yet he opened my eyes. We know that God does not listen to sinners, but if anyone is a worshiper of God and does his will, God listens to him. Never since the world began has it been heard that anyone opened the eyes of a man born blind. If this man were not from God, he could do nothing." They answered him, "You were born in utter sin, and would you teach us?" And they cast him out.

Jesus heard that they had cast him out, and having found him he said, "Do you believe in the Son of Man?" He answered, "And who is he, sir, that I may believe in him?" Jesus said to him, "You have seen him, and it is he who is speaking to you." He said, "Lord, I believe," and he worshiped him.

Jesus said, "For judgment I came into this world, that those who do not see may see, and those who see may become blind." Some of the Pharisees near him heard these things, and said to him, "Are we also blind?" Jesus said to them, "If you were blind, you would have no guilt; but now that you say, 'We see,' your guilt remains.

"Truly, truly, I say to you,
he who does not enter the sheepfold by the door
but climbs in by another way,
that man is a thief and a robber.
But he who enters by the door is the shepherd of the sheep.
To him the gatekeeper opens.
The sheep hear his voice, and he calls his own sheep by name
and leads them out.
When he has brought out all his own, he goes before them,
and the sheep follow him, for they know his voice.
A stranger they will not follow, but they will flee from him,
for they do not know the voice of strangers."

This figure of speech Jesus used with them, but they did not understand what he was saying to them. So Jesus again said to them,
"Truly, truly, I say to you,
I am the door of the sheep.

"All who came before me are thieves and robbers,
but the sheep did not listen to them.
I am the door.
If anyone enters by me, he will be saved
and will go in and out and find pasture.
The thief comes only to steal and kill and destroy.

"I came that they may have life
and have it abundantly.

"I am the good shepherd.
The good shepherd lays down his life for the sheep.
He who is a hired hand and not a shepherd, who does not own the sheep,
sees the wolf coming and leaves the sheep and flees,
and the wolf snatches them and scatters them.
He flees because he is a hired hand and cares nothing for the sheep.
I am the good shepherd.
I know my own and my own know me,
just as the Father knows me and I know the Father;
and I lay down my life for the sheep.
And I have other sheep that are not of this fold.
I must bring them also, and they will listen to my voice.
So there will be one flock, one shepherd.
For this reason the Father loves me,
because I lay down my life that I may take it up again.
No one takes it from me, but I lay it down of my own accord.
I have authority to lay it down, and I have authority to take it up again.
This charge I have received from my Father."

There was again a division among 'the Jews' because of these words. Many of them said, "He has a demon, and is insane; why listen to him?" Others said, "These are not the words of one who is oppressed by a demon. Can a demon open the eyes of the blind?"

At that time the Feast of Dedication took place at Jerusalem.

It was winter, and Jesus was walking in the temple, in the colonnade of Solomon. So 'the Jews' gathered around him and said to him, "How long will you keep us in suspense? If you are the Christ, tell us plainly."

Jesus answered them, "I told you, and you do not believe. The works that I do in my Father's name bear witness about me, but you do not believe because you are not part of my flock.
My sheep hear my voice, and I know them, and they follow me.
I give them eternal life, and they will never perish,
and no one will snatch them out of my hand.
My Father, who has given them to me, is greater than all,
and no one is able to snatch them out of the Father's hand.
I and the Father are one."

'The Jews' picked up stones again to stone him. Jesus answered them, "I have shown you many good works from the Father; for which of them are you going to stone me?" 'The Jews' answered him, "It is not for a good work that we are going to stone you but for blasphemy, because you, being a man, make yourself God." Jesus answered them, "Is it not written in your Law, 'I said, you are gods'? If he called them gods to whom the word of God came – and Scripture cannot be broken – do you say of him whom the Father consecrated and sent into the world, 'You are blaspheming,' because I said, 'I am the Son of God'? If I am not doing the works of my Father, then do not believe me; but if I do them, even though you do not believe me, believe the works, that you may know and understand that the Father is in me and I am in the Father."

Again they sought to arrest him, but he escaped from their hands.

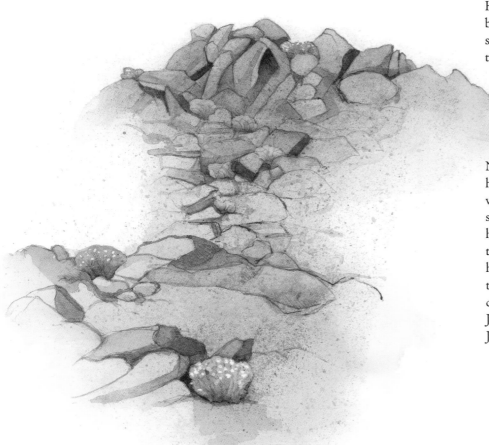

He went away again across the Jordan to the place where John had been baptizing at first, and there he remained. And many came to him. And they said, "John did no sign, but everything that John said about this man was true." And many believed in him there.

Now a certain man was ill, Lazarus of Bethany, the village of Mary and her sister Martha. It was Mary who anointed the Lord with ointment and wiped his feet with her hair, whose brother Lazarus was ill. So the sisters sent to him, saying, "Lord, he whom you love is ill." But when Jesus heard it he said, "This illness does not lead to death. It is for the glory of God, so that the Son of God may be glorified through it." Now Jesus loved Martha and her sister and Lazarus. So, when he heard that Lazarus was ill, he stayed two days longer in the place where he was. Then after this he said to the disciples, "Let us go to Judea again." The disciples said to him, "Rabbi, 'the Jews' were just now seeking to stone you, and are you going there again?" Jesus answered,

"Are there not twelve hours in the day?
If anyone walks in the day, he does not stumble,
because he sees the light of this world.
But if anyone walks in the night, he stumbles,
because the light is not in him."

After saying these things, he said to them, "Our friend Lazarus has fallen asleep, but I go to awaken him." The disciples said to him, "Lord, if he has fallen asleep, he will recover[8]." Now Jesus had spoken of his death, but they thought that he meant taking rest in sleep. Then Jesus told them plainly, "Lazarus has died, and for your sake I am glad that I was not there, so that you may believe. But let us go to him." So Thomas, called the Twin, said to his fellow disciples, "Let us also go, that we may die with him."

Now when Jesus came, he found that Lazarus had already been in the tomb four days. Bethany was near Jerusalem, about two miles off, and many of 'the Jews' had come to Martha and Mary to console them concerning their brother. So when Martha heard that Jesus was coming, she went and met him, but Mary remained seated in the house. Martha said to Jesus, "Lord, if you had been here, my brother would not have died. But even now I know that whatever you ask from God, God will give you."

Jesus said to her, "Your brother will rise again." Martha said to him, "I know that he will rise again in the resurrection on the last day." Jesus said to her,

"I am the resurrection and the life.

Whoever believes in me, though he die,

yet shall he live,

and everyone who lives and believes in me

shall never die.

"Do you believe this?" She said to him, "Yes, Lord; I believe that you are the Christ, the Son of God, who is coming into the world."

When she had said this, she went and called her sister Mary, saying in private, "The Teacher is here and is calling for you." And when she heard it, she rose quickly and went to him. Now Jesus had not yet come into the village, but was still in the place where Martha had met him. When 'the Jews' who were with her in the house, consoling her, saw Mary rise quickly and go out, they followed her, supposing that she was going to the tomb to weep there.

Now when Mary came to where Jesus was and saw him, she fell at his feet, saying to him, "Lord, if you had been here, my brother would not have died." When Jesus saw her weeping, and 'the Jews' who had come with her also weeping, he was deeply moved in his spirit and greatly troubled[9]. And he said, "Where have you laid him?" They said to him, "Lord, come and see." Jesus wept. So 'the Jews' said, "See how he loved him!" But some of them said, "Could not he who opened the eyes of the blind man also have kept this man from dying?"

Then Jesus, deeply moved again, came to the tomb. It was a cave, and a stone lay against it. Jesus said, "Take away the stone." Martha, the sister of the dead man, said to him, "Lord, by this time there will be an odour, for he has been dead four days." Jesus said to her, "Did I not tell you that if you believed you would see the glory of God?" So they took away the stone.

And Jesus lifted up his eyes and said, "Father, I thank you that you have heard me. I knew that you always hear me, but I said this on account of the people standing around, that they may believe that you sent me." When he had said these things, he cried out with a loud voice, "Lazarus, come out." The man who had died came out, his hands and feet bound with linen strips, and his face wrapped with a cloth. Jesus said to them,

"Unbind him, and let him go."

John 11:38-44

Many of 'the Jews' therefore, who had come with Mary and had seen what he did, believed in him, but some of them went to the Pharisees and told them what Jesus had done. So the chief priests and the Pharisees gathered the Council and said, "What are we to do? For this man performs many signs. If we let him go on like this, everyone will believe in him, and the Romans will come and take away both our place[10] and our nation."

But one of them, Caiaphas, who was high priest that year, said to them, "You know nothing at all. Nor do you understand that it is better for you that one man should die for the people, not that the whole nation should perish." He did not say this of his own accord, but being high priest that year he prophesied that Jesus would die for the nation, and not for the nation only, but also to gather into one the children of God who are scattered abroad.

So from that day on they made plans to put him to death.

Jesus therefore no longer walked openly among 'the Jews', but went from there to the region near the wilderness, to a town called Ephraim, and there he stayed with the disciples.

Now the Passover of the Jews was at hand,

and many went up from the country to Jerusalem before the Passover to purify themselves. They were looking for Jesus and saying to one another as they stood in the temple, "What do you think? That he will not come to the feast at all?" Now the chief priests and the Pharisees had given orders that if anyone knew where he was, he should let them know, so that they might arrest him.

Six days before the Passover,

Jesus therefore came to Bethany, where Lazarus was, whom Jesus had raised from the dead. So they gave a dinner for him there. Martha served, and Lazarus was one of those reclining with him at table. Mary therefore took [about 300 grams] of expensive ointment made from pure nard, and anointed the feet of Jesus and wiped his feet with her hair. The house was filled with the fragrance of the perfume. But Judas Iscariot, one of his disciples (he who was about to betray him), said, "Why was this ointment not sold for three hundred denarii and given to the poor?" He said this, not because he cared about the poor, but because he was a thief, and having charge of the moneybag he used to help himself to what was put into it. Jesus said, "Leave her alone, so that she may keep it for the day of my burial. For the poor you always have with you, but you do not always have me."

When the large crowd of 'the Jews' learned that Jesus was there, they came, not only on account of him but also to see Lazarus, whom he had raised from the dead. So the chief priests made plans to put Lazarus to death as well, because on account of him many of 'the Jews' were going away and believing in Jesus.

The next day

the large crowd that had come to the feast heard that Jesus was coming to Jerusalem. So they took branches of palm trees and went out to meet him, crying out, "Hosanna! Blessed is he who comes in the name of the Lord, even the King of Israel!" And Jesus found a young donkey and sat on it, just as it is written,

> "Fear not, daughter of Zion;
> behold, your king is coming,
> sitting on a donkey's colt!"

His disciples did not understand these things at first, but when Jesus was glorified, then they remembered that these things had been written about him and had been done to him. The crowd that had been with him when he called Lazarus out of the tomb and raised him from the dead continued to bear witness. The reason why the crowd went to meet him was that they heard he had done this sign. So the Pharisees said to one another "You see that you are gaining nothing. Look, the world has gone after him."

Now among those who went up to worship at the feast were some Greeks. So these came to Philip, who was from Bethsaida in Galilee, and asked him, "Sir, we wish to see Jesus." Philip went and told Andrew; Andrew and Philip went and told Jesus. And Jesus answered them, "The hour has come for the Son of Man to be glorified.

> **Truly, truly, I say to you,**
> unless a grain of wheat falls into the earth and dies, it remains alone;
> but if it dies, it bears much fruit.

"Whoever loves his life loses it, and whoever hates his life in this world will keep it for eternal life. If anyone serves me, he must follow me; and where I am, there will my servant be also. If anyone serves me, the Father will honour him.

"Now is my soul troubled. And what shall I say? 'Father, save me from this hour'? But for this purpose I have come to this hour. Father, glorify your name."

Then a voice came from heaven: "I have glorified it, and I will glorify it again." The crowd that stood there and heard it said that it had thundered. Others said, "An angel has spoken to him." Jesus answered, "This voice has come for your sake, not mine.

Now is the judgment of this world;

now will the ruler of this world be cast out.

And I, when I am lifted up from the earth,

will draw all people to myself."

He said this to show by what kind of death he was going to die.

So the crowd answered him, "We have heard from the Law that the Christ remains forever. How can you say that the Son of Man must be lifted up? Who is this Son of Man?" So Jesus said to them,
"The light is among you for a little while longer.
Walk while you have the light, lest darkness overtake you.
The one who walks in the darkness does not know where he is going.
While you have the light, believe in the light,
that you may become sons of light."

When Jesus had said these things, he departed and hid himself from them.

Though he had done so many signs before them, they still did not believe in him, so that the word spoken by the prophet Isaiah might be fulfilled:
"Lord, who has believed what he heard from us,
and to whom has the arm of the Lord been revealed?"

Therefore they could not believe. For again Isaiah said,
"He has blinded their eyes
and hardened their heart,
lest they see with their eyes,
and understand with their heart, and turn,
and I would heal them."

Isaiah said these things because he saw his glory and spoke of him. Nevertheless, many even of the authorities believed in him, but for fear of the Pharisees they did not confess it, so that they would not be put out of the synagogue; for they loved the glory that comes from man more than the glory that comes from God.

And Jesus cried out and said,

*"Whoever believes in me, believes not in me
but in him who sent me.
And whoever sees me sees him who sent me.
I have come into the world as light,
so that whoever believes in me
may not remain in darkness.*

If anyone hears my words and does not keep them, I do not judge him; for I did not come to judge the world but to save the world. The one who rejects me and does not receive my words has a judge; the word that I have spoken will judge him on the last day. For I have not spoken on my own authority, but the Father who sent me has himself given me a commandment—what to say and what to speak. And I know that his commandment is eternal life. What I say, therefore, I say as the Father has told me."

Now before the Feast of the Passover, when

Jesus knew that his hour had come

to depart out of this world to the Father,

having loved his own in the world,

he loved them to the end.

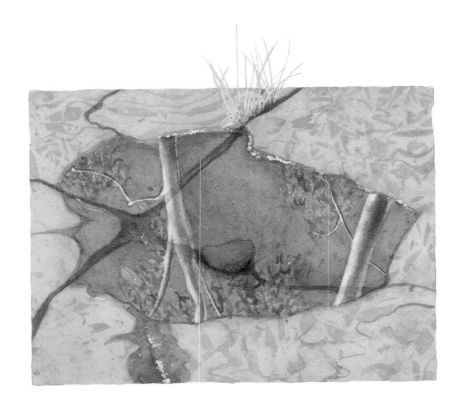

John 13:1

During supper, when the devil had already put it into the heart of Judas Iscariot, Simon's son, to betray him, Jesus, knowing that the Father had given all things into his hands, and that he had come from God and was going back to God, rose from supper. He laid aside his outer garments, and taking a towel, tied it around his waist. Then he poured water into a basin and began to wash the disciples' feet and to wipe them with the towel that was wrapped around him.

He came to Simon Peter, who said to him, "Lord, do you wash my feet?" Jesus answered him, "What I am doing you do not understand now, but afterward you will understand." Peter said to him, "You shall never wash my feet." Jesus answered him, "If I do not wash you, you have no share with me." Simon Peter said to him, "Lord, not my feet only but also my hands and my head!" Jesus said to him, "The one who has bathed does not need to wash, except for his feet, but is completely clean. And *you* are clean, but not every one of *you*." For he knew who was to betray him; that was why he said, "Not all of you are clean."

When he had washed their feet and put on his outer garments and resumed his place, he said to them, "Do you understand what I have done to you? You call me Teacher and Lord, and you are right, for so I am. If I then, your Lord and Teacher, have washed your feet, you also ought to wash one another's feet. For I have given you an example, that you also should do just as I have done to you.

Truly, truly, I say to you,
a servant is not greater than his master,
nor is a messenger greater than the one who sent him.
If you know these things, blessed are you if you do them.

"I am not speaking of all of you; I know whom I have chosen. But the Scripture will be fulfilled, 'He who ate my bread has lifted his heel against me.' I am telling you this now, before it takes place, that when it does take place you may believe that *I am.*

> *Truly, truly, I say to you,*
> whoever receives the one I send receives me,
> and whoever receives me receives the one who sent me."

After saying these things, Jesus was troubled in his spirit, and testified,
"*Truly, truly, I say to you*, one of you will betray me."

The disciples looked at one another, uncertain of whom he spoke. One of his disciples, whom Jesus loved, was reclining at table close to Jesus, so Simon Peter motioned to him to ask Jesus of whom he was speaking. So that disciple, leaning back against Jesus, said to him, "Lord, who is it?" Jesus answered, "It is he to whom I will give this morsel of bread when I have dipped it." So when he had dipped the morsel, he gave it to Judas, the son of Simon Iscariot. Then after he had taken the morsel, Satan entered into him. Jesus said to him, "What you are going to do, do quickly." Now no one at the table knew why he said this to him. Some thought that, because Judas had the moneybag, Jesus was telling him, "Buy what we need for the feast," or that he should give something to the poor. So, after receiving the morsel of bread, he immediately went out. **And it was night.**

When he had gone out, Jesus said,

"Now is the Son of Man glorified,

and God is glorified in him.
If God is glorified in him,
God will also glorify him in himself,
and glorify him at once.

"Little children, yet a little while I am with you. You will seek me, and just as I said to 'the Jews', so now I also say to you, 'Where I am going you cannot come.'

"A new commandment I give to you, that you love one another: just as I have loved you, you also are to love one another. By this all people will know that you are my disciples, if you have love for one another."

Simon Peter said to him, "Lord, where are you going?" Jesus answered him, "Where I am going you cannot follow me now, but you will follow afterward." Peter said to him, "Lord, why can I not follow you now? I will lay down my life for you." Jesus answered, "Will you lay down your life for me?
Truly, truly, I say to you,
the rooster will not crow till you have denied me three times.

"Let not your hearts be troubled.

Believe in God; believe also in me. In my Father's home[f] are many abiding places[g]. If it were not so, would I have told you that I go to prepare a place for you? And if I go and prepare a place for you, I will come again and will take you to myself, that where I am you may be also. And you know the way to where I am going."

Thomas said to him, "Lord, we do not know where you are going. **How can we know the way?"** Jesus said to him,

"I am the way, and the truth, and the life.
No one comes to the Father except through me.

"If you had known me, you would have known my Father also. From now on you do know him and have seen him."

Philip said to him, "Lord, show us the Father, and it is enough for us."

Jesus said to him, "Have I been with you so long, and you still do not know me, Philip? Whoever has seen me has seen the Father. How can you say, 'Show us the Father'? Do you not believe that I am in the Father and the Father is in me? The words that I say to you I do not speak on my own authority, but the Father who dwells in me does his works. Believe me that I am in the Father and the Father is in me, or else believe on account of the works themselves.

"Truly, truly, I say to you,
whoever believes in me will also do the works that I do;
and greater works than these will he do,
because I am going to the Father.

John 14:1-12

"Whatever you ask in my name, this I will do, that the Father may be glorified in the Son. If you ask me anything in my name, I will do it. If you love me, you will keep my commandments. And I will ask the Father, and he will give you another Helper/Paraclete[11], to be with you forever, even the Spirit of truth, whom the world cannot receive, because it neither sees him nor knows him. You know him, for he dwells with you and will be in you. I will not leave you as orphans; I will come to you. Yet a little while and the world will see me no more, but you will see me. Because I live, you also will live. In that day you will know that I am in my Father, and you in me, and I in you.

"Whoever has my commandments and keeps them, he it is who loves me. And he who loves me will be loved by my Father, and I will love him and manifest myself to him."

Judas (not Iscariot) said to him, "Lord, how is it that you will manifest yourself to us, and not to the world?" Jesus answered him, "If anyone loves me, he will keep my word, and my Father will love him, and we will come to him and make our home[f] with him. Whoever does not love me does not keep my words. And the word that you hear is not mine but the Father's who sent me. These things I have spoken to you while I am still with you. But the Helper, the Holy Spirit, whom the Father will send in my name, he will teach you all things and bring to your remembrance all that I have said to you.

"Peace I leave with you; my peace I give to you. Not as the world gives do I give to you.

Let not your hearts be troubled, neither let them be afraid.

"You heard me say to you, 'I am going away, and I will come to you.' If you loved me, you would have rejoiced, because I am going to the Father, for the Father is greater than I. And now I have told you before it takes place, so that when it does take place you may believe.

"I will no longer talk much with you, for the ruler of this world is coming. He has no claim on me, but I do as the Father has commanded me, so that the world may know that I love the Father.

"Rise, let us go from here.

*"I am the true vine,
and my Father is the vinedresser.*

"Every branch in me that does not bear fruit he takes away,
and every branch that does bear fruit he prunes,
that it may bear more fruit.
Already you are clean because of the word that I have spoken to you. Abide
in me, and I in you. As the branch cannot bear fruit by itself, unless it abides
in the vine, neither can you, unless you abide in me.

"I am the vine; you are the branches.
Whoever abides in me and I in him, he it is that bears much fruit,
for apart from me you can do nothing.
If anyone does not abide in me he is thrown away like a branch and withers;
and the branches are gathered, thrown into the fire, and burned.

"If you abide in me, and my words abide in you, ask whatever you wish, and
it will be done for you. By this my Father is glorified, that you bear much
fruit and so prove to be my disciples. As the Father has loved me, so have I
loved you. Abide in my love. If you keep my commandments, you will abide
in my love, just as I have kept my Father's commandments and abide in his
love.

*"These things I have spoken to you,
that my joy may be in you,
and that your joy may be full.*

*"This is my commandment,
that you love one another
as I have loved you.*

"Greater love has no one than this, that someone lay down his life for his friends. You are my friends if you do what I command you. No longer do I call you servants, for the servant does not know what his master is doing; but I have called you friends, for all that I have heard from my Father I have made known to you.

"You did not choose me, but I chose you and appointed you that you should go and bear fruit and that your fruit should abide, so that whatever you ask the Father in my name, he may give it to you. These things I command you, so that you will love one another.

"If the world hates you, know that it has hated me before it hated you. If you were of the world, the world would love you as its own; but because you are not of the world, but I chose you out of the world, therefore the world hates you. Remember the word that I said to you: 'A servant is not greater than his master.' If they persecuted me, they will also persecute you. If they kept my word, they will also keep yours. But all these things they will do to you on account of my name, because they do not know him who sent me. If I had not come and spoken to them, they would not have been guilty of sin, but now they have no excuse for their sin. Whoever hates me hates my Father also. If I had not done among them the works that no one else did, they would not be guilty of sin, but now they have seen and hated both me and my Father. But the word that is written in their Law must be fulfilled: 'They hated me without a cause.'

"But when the Helper comes, whom I will send to you from the Father, the Spirit of truth, who proceeds from the Father, he will bear witness about me. And you also will bear witness, because you have been with me from the beginning. I have said all these things to you to keep you from falling away. They will put you out of the synagogues. Indeed, the hour is coming when whoever kills you will think he is offering service to God. And they will do these things because they have not known the Father, nor me. But I have said these things to you, that when their hour comes you may remember that I told them to you.

"I did not say these things to you from the beginning, because I was with you. But now I am going to him who sent me, and none of you asks me, 'Where are you going?' But because I have said these things to you, sorrow has filled your heart. Nevertheless, I tell you the truth: it is to your advantage that I go away, for if I do not go away, the Helper will not come to you. But if I go, I will send him to you. And when he comes, he will convict the world concerning sin and righteousness and judgment: concerning sin, because they do not believe in me; concerning righteousness, because I go to the Father, and you will see me no longer; concerning judgment, because the ruler of this world is judged. I still have many things to say to you, but you cannot bear them now. When the Spirit of truth comes, he will guide you in^h all the truth, for he will not speak on his own authority, but whatever he hears he will speak, and he will declare to you the things that are to come. He will glorify me, for he will take what is mine and declare it to you. All that the Father has is mine; therefore I said that he will take what is mine and declare it to you.

"A little while, and you will see me no longer; and again a little while, and you will see me." So some of his disciples said to one another, "What is this that he says to us, 'A little while, and you will not see me, and again a little while, and you will see me'; and, 'because I am going to the Father'?" So they were saying, "What does he mean by 'a little while'? We do not know what he is talking about." Jesus knew that they wanted to ask him, so he said to them, "Is this what you are asking yourselves, what I meant by saying, 'A little while and you will not see me, and again a little while and you will see me'?

Truly, truly, I say to you,

you will weep and lament, but the world will rejoice.

You will be sorrowful, but your sorrow will turn into joy. When a woman is giving birth, she has sorrow because her hour has come, but when she has delivered the baby, she no longer remembers the anguish, for joy that a human being has been born into the world. So also you have sorrow now, but I will see you again, and your hearts will rejoice, and no one will take your joy from you. In that day you will ask nothing of me.

Truly, truly, I say to you,

whatever you ask of the Father in my name, he will give it to you.

Until now you have asked nothing in my name.

Ask, and you will receive, that your joy may be full.

I have said these things to you in figures of speech. The hour is coming when I will no longer speak to you in figures of speech but will tell you plainly about the Father. In that day you will ask in my name, and I do not say to you that I will ask the Father on your behalf; for the Father himself loves you, because you have loved me and have believed that I came from God.

"I came from the Father and have come into the world, and now I am leaving the world and going to the Father." His disciples said, "Ah, now you are speaking plainly and not using figurative speech! Now we know that you know all things and do not need anyone to question you; this is why we believe that you came from God." Jesus answered them, "Do you now believe? Behold, the hour is coming, indeed it has come, when you will be scattered, each to his own home, and will leave me alone. Yet I am not alone, for the Father is with me.

"I have said these things to you,
that in me you may have peace.
In the world you will have tribulation.
But take heart;

I have overcome the world."

When Jesus had spoken these words he lifted up his eyes to heaven, and said, "Father, the hour has come;

glorify your Son that the Son may glorify you,
since you have given him authority over all flesh,
to give eternal life to all whom you have given him.

And this is eternal life:

that they know you the only true God,

and Jesus Christ whom you have sent.

"I glorified you on earth, having accomplished the work that you gave me to do. And now,

"Father, glorify me in your own presence with the glory that I had with you before the world existed.

"I have manifested your name to the people whom you gave me out of the world. Yours they were, and you gave them to me, and they have kept your word. Now they know that everything that you have given me is from you. For I have given them the words that you gave me, and they have received them and have come to know in truth that I came from you; and they have believed that you sent me.

John 17:1-8

"I am praying for them. I am not praying for the world but for those whom you have given me, for they are yours. All mine are yours, and yours are mine, and I am glorified in them. And I am no longer in the world, but they are in the world, and I am coming to you.

> "*Holy Father, keep them in your name, which you have given me, that they may be one, even as we are one.* While I was with them, I kept them in your name, which you have given me. I have guarded them, and not one of them has been lost except the son of destruction, that the Scripture might be fulfilled.

> "But now I am coming to you, and these things I speak in the world, that they may have my joy fulfilled in themselves. I have given them your word, and the world has hated them because they are not of the world, just as I am not of the world.

> "*I do not ask that you take them out of the world, but that you keep them from the evil one.* They are not of the world, just as I am not of the world.

> "*Sanctify them in the truth;* your word is truth. As you sent me into the world, so I have sent them into the world. And for their sake I consecrate/sanctify myself that they also may be sanctified in truth.

"I do not ask for these only, but also for those who will believe in me through their word,

> "*that they may all be one*, just as you, Father, are in me, and I in you, that they also may be in us, so that the world may believe that you have sent me.

> "The glory that you have given me I have given to them, *that they may be one even as we are one, I in them and you in me, that they may become perfectly one, so that the world may know that you sent me and loved them even as you loved me.*

> "*Father, I desire that they also, whom you have given me, may be with me where I am, to see my glory that you have given me because you loved me before the foundation of the world.*

"O righteous Father, even though the world does not know you, I know you, and these know that you have sent me. I made known to them your name, and I will continue to make it known, that the love with which you have loved me may be in them, and I in them."

When Jesus had spoken these words, he went out with his disciples across the Kidron Valley, where there was a garden, which he and his disciples entered.

Now Judas, who betrayed him, also knew the place, for Jesus often met there with his disciples. So Judas, having procured a band of soldiers and some officers from the chief priests and the Pharisees, went there with lanterns and torches and weapons. Then Jesus, knowing all that would happen to him, came forward and said to them, *"Whom do you seek?"* They answered him, "Jesus of Nazareth." Jesus said to them, *"I am."* Judas, who betrayed him, was standing with them. When Jesus said to them, *"I am,"* they drew back and fell to the ground. So he asked them again, *"Whom do you seek?"* And they said, "Jesus of Nazareth." Jesus answered, "I told you that *I am.* So, if you seek me, let these men go." This was to fulfil the word that he had spoken: "Of those whom you gave me I have lost not one." Then Simon Peter, having a sword, drew it and struck the high priest's servant and cut off his right ear. (The servant's name was Malchus.) So Jesus said to Peter, "Put your sword into its sheath; shall I not drink the cup that the Father has given me?"

So the band of soldiers and their captain and the officers of 'the Jews' arrested Jesus and bound him.

First they led him to Annas, for he was the father-in-law of Caiaphas, who was high priest that year. It was Caiaphas who had advised 'the Jews' that it would be expedient that one man should die for the people. Simon Peter followed Jesus, and so did another disciple. Since that disciple was known to the high priest, he entered with Jesus into the court of the high priest, but Peter stood outside at the door. So the other disciple, who was known to the high priest, went out and spoke to the servant girl who kept watch at the door, and brought Peter in. The servant girl at the door said to Peter, "You also are not one of this man's disciples, are you?" He said, "I am not." Now the servants and officers had made a charcoal fire, because it was cold, and they were standing and warming themselves. Peter also was with them, standing and warming himself.

The high priest then questioned Jesus about his disciples and his teaching. Jesus answered him, "I have spoken openly to the world. I have always taught in synagogues and in the temple, where all Jews come together. I have said nothing in secret. Why do you ask me? Ask those who have heard me what I said to them; they know what I said." When he had said these things, one of the officers standing by struck Jesus with his hand, saying, "Is that how you answer the high priest?" Jesus answered him, "If what I said is wrong, bear witness about the wrong; but if what I said is right, why do you strike me?"

Annas then sent him bound to Caiaphas the high priest. Now Simon Peter was standing and warming himself. So they said to him, "You also are not one of his disciples, are you?" He denied it and said, "I am not." One of the servants of the high priest, a relative of the man whose ear Peter had cut off, asked, "Did I not see you in the garden with him?" Peter again denied it, and at once a rooster crowed.

Then they led Jesus from the house of Caiaphas to the governor's headquarters. **It was early morning.**

They themselves did not enter the governor's headquarters, so that they would not be defiled, but could eat the Passover. So Pilate went outside to them and said, "What accusation do you bring against this man?" They answered him, "If this man were not doing evil, we would not have delivered him over to you." Pilate said to them, "Take him yourselves and judge him by your own law." The Jews' said to him, "It is not lawful for us to put anyone to death." This was to fulfil the word that Jesus had spoken to show by what kind of death he was going to die.

So Pilate entered his headquarters again and called Jesus and said to him, "Are you the King of the Jews?" Jesus answered, "Do you say this of your own accord, or did others say it to you about me?" Pilate answered, "Am I a Jew? Your own nation and the chief priests have delivered you over to me. What have you done?" Jesus answered, "My kingdom is not of this world. If my kingdom were of this world, my servants would have been fighting, that I might not be delivered over to the Jews. But my kingdom is not from the world." Then Pilate said to him, "So you are a king?" Jesus answered, "You say that I am a king. For this purpose I was born and for this purpose I have come into the world— to bear witness to the truth. Everyone who is of the truth listens to my voice." Pilate said to him, "What is truth?"

After he had said this, he went back outside to 'the Jews' and told them,

"I find no guilt in him."

But you have a custom that I should release one man for you at the Passover. So do you want me to release to you the King of the Jews?" They cried out again, "Not this man, but Barabbas!" Now Barabbas was a robber.

Then Pilate took Jesus and flogged him. And the soldiers twisted together a crown of thorns and put it on his head and arrayed him in a purple robe. They came up to him, saying, "Hail, King of the Jews!" and struck him with their hands.

Pilate went out again and said to them, "See, I am bringing him out to you that you may know that

I find no guilt in him."

So Jesus came out, wearing the crown of thorns and the purple robe. Pilate said to them, **"Behold the man!"**

When the chief priests and the officers saw him, they cried out, "Crucify him, crucify him!" Pilate said to them, "Take him yourselves and crucify him, for

I find no guilt in him."

'The Jews' answered him, "We have a law, and according to that law he ought to die because he has made himself the Son of God."

When Pilate heard this statement, he was even more afraid. He entered his headquarters again and said to Jesus, "Where are you from?" But Jesus gave him no answer. So Pilate said to him, "You will not speak to me? Do you not know that I have authority to release you and authority to crucify you?" Jesus answered him, "You would have no authority over me at all unless it had been given you from above. Therefore he who delivered me over to you has the greater sin." From then on Pilate sought to release him, but 'the Jews' cried out, "If you release this man, you are not Caesar's friend. Everyone who makes himself a king opposes Caesar." So when Pilate heard these words, he brought Jesus out and sat down on the judgment seat at a place called The Stone Pavement, and in Aramaic Gabbatha.

Now it was the day of
Preparation of the Passover.

It was about the sixth hour. He said to 'the Jews',

"Behold your King!"

They cried out, "Away with him, away with him, crucify him!" Pilate said to them, "Shall I crucify your King?" The chief priests answered, "We have no king but Caesar." So he delivered him over to them to be crucified.

So they took Jesus, and he went out, bearing his own cross, to the place called The Place of a Skull, which in Aramaic is called Golgotha. There they crucified him, and with him two others, one on either side, and Jesus between them. Pilate also wrote an inscription and put it on the cross. It read,

"Jesus of Nazareth, the King of the Jews."

Many of 'the Jews' read this inscription, for the place where Jesus was crucified was near the city, and it was written in Aramaic, in Latin, and in Greek. So the chief priests of 'the Jews' said to Pilate, "Do not write, 'The King of the Jews,' but rather, 'This man said, I am King of the Jews.'" Pilate answered, "What I have written I have written."

When the soldiers had crucified Jesus, they took his garments and divided them into four parts, one part for each soldier; also his tunic. But the tunic was seamless, woven in one piece from top to bottom, so they said to one another, "Let us not tear it, but cast lots for it to see whose it shall be." This was to fulfil the Scripture which says,

"They divided my garments among them,
and for my clothing they cast lots."

So the soldiers did these things, but standing by the cross of Jesus were his mother and his mother's sister, Mary the wife of Clopas, and Mary Magdalene. When Jesus saw his mother and the disciple whom he loved standing nearby, he said to his mother, "Woman, behold, your son!" Then he said to the disciple, "Behold, your mother!" And from that hour the disciple took her to his own home.

After this, Jesus, knowing that all was now accomplished/fulfilled/completed[12], said (to fulfil the Scripture), "I thirst." A jar full of sour wine stood there, so they put a sponge full of the sour wine on a hyssop branch and held it to his mouth. When Jesus had received the sour wine, he said, "It is accomplished[12]," and he bowed his head and handed over[j] his spirit.

and so that the bodies would not remain on the cross on the Sabbath (for that Sabbath was a high day), 'the Jews' asked Pilate that their legs might be broken and that they might be taken away. So the soldiers came and broke the legs of the first, and of the other who had been crucified with him. But when they came to Jesus and saw that he was already dead, they did not break his legs. But one of the soldiers pierced his side with a spear, and at once there came out blood and water. He who saw it has borne witness— his testimony is true, and he knows that he is telling the truth— that you also may believe. For these things took place that the Scripture might be fulfilled:

"Not one of his bones will be broken."

And again another Scripture says,
"They will look on him whom they have pierced."

After these things Joseph of Arimathea, who was a disciple of Jesus, but secretly for fear of 'the Jews', asked Pilate that he might take away the body of Jesus, and Pilate gave him permission. So he came and took away his body. Nicodemus also, who earlier had come to Jesus by night, came bringing a mixture of myrrh and aloes, [about thirty three kilos] in weight. So they took the body of Jesus and bound it in linen cloths with the spices, as is the burial custom of the Jews. Now in the place where he was crucified there was a garden, and in the garden a new tomb in which no one had yet been laid. So because of the Jewish day of Preparation, since the tomb was close at hand, they laid Jesus there.

Now on the first day of the week Mary Magdalene came to the tomb early, while it was still dark,

and saw that the stone had been taken away from the tomb. So she ran and went to Simon Peter and the other disciple, the one whom Jesus loved, and said to them, "They have taken the Lord out of the tomb, and we do not know where they have laid him."

So Peter went out with the other disciple, and they were going toward the tomb. Both of them were running together, but the other disciple outran Peter and reached the tomb first. And stooping to look in, he saw the linen cloths lying there, but he did not go in. Then Simon Peter came, following him, and went into the tomb. He saw the linen cloths lying there, and the face cloth, which had been on Jesus' head, not lying with the linen cloths but folded up in a place by itself. Then the other disciple, who had reached the tomb first, also went in, and he saw and believed; for as yet they did not understand the Scripture, that he must rise from the dead. Then the disciples went back to their homes.

But Mary stood weeping outside the tomb, and as she wept she stooped to look into the tomb. And she saw two angels in white, sitting where the body of Jesus had lain, one at the head and one at the feet. They said to her, "Woman, why are you weeping?" She said to them, "They have taken away my Lord, and I do not know where they have laid him." Having said this, she turned around and saw Jesus standing, but she did not know that it was Jesus. Jesus said to her, "Woman, why are you weeping? *Whom are you seeking?*"

Supposing him to be the gardener, she said to him, "Sir, if you have carried him away, tell me where you have laid him, and I will take him away." Jesus said to her, "Mary." She turned and said to him in Aramaic, "Rabboni!" (which means Teacher). Jesus said to her, "Do not cling to me, for I have not yet ascended to the Father; but go to my brothers and say to them, 'I am ascending to my Father and your Father, to my God and your God.'"

Mary Magdalene went and announced to the disciples, "I have seen the Lord" – and that he had said these things to her.

On the evening of that day,
the first day of the week,

the doors being locked where the disciples were for fear of 'the Jews', Jesus came and stood among them and said to them,

"Peace be with you."

When he had said this, he showed them his hands and his side. Then the disciples were overjoyed[k] when they saw the Lord. Jesus said to them again,

"Peace be with you.

"As the Father has sent me even so I am sending you." And when he had said this, he breathed on them and said to them, "Receive the Holy Spirit. If you forgive the sins of any, they are forgiven them; if you withhold forgiveness from any, it is withheld."

Now Thomas, one of the Twelve, called the Twin, was not with them when Jesus came. So the other disciples told him, "We have seen the Lord." But he said to them, "Unless I see in his hands the mark of the nails, and place my finger into the mark of the nails, and place my hand into his side, I will never believe."

Eight days later, his disciples were inside again, and Thomas was with them. Although the doors were locked, Jesus came and stood among them and said,

"Peace be with you."

Then he said to Thomas, "Put your finger here, and see my hands; and put out your hand, and place it in my side. Do not disbelieve, but believe." Thomas answered him, "My Lord and my God!" Jesus said to him, "Have you believed because you have seen me?

Blessed are those who have not seen
and yet have believed."

Now Jesus did many other signs in the presence of the disciples,

which are not written in this book;

but these are written so that you may believe

that Jesus is the Christ, the Son of God,

and that by believing

you may have life in his name.

After this Jesus revealed himself again to the disciples by the Sea of Tiberias, and he revealed himself in this way.

Simon Peter, Thomas (called the Twin), Nathanael of Cana in Galilee, the sons of Zebedee, and two others of his disciples were together. Simon Peter said to them, "I am going fishing." They said to him, "We will go with you." They went out and got into the boat, but that night they caught nothing.

Just as day was breaking,

Jesus stood on the shore; yet the disciples did not know that it was Jesus. Jesus said to them, "Children, do you have any fish?" They answered him, "No." He said to them, "Cast the net on the right side of the boat, and you will find some." So they cast it, and now they were not able to haul it in, because of the quantity of fish. That disciple whom Jesus loved therefore said to Peter, "It is the Lord!" When Simon Peter heard that it was the Lord, he put on his outer garment, for he was stripped for work, and threw himself into the sea. The other disciples came in the boat, dragging the net full of fish, for they were not far from the land, but about a hundred yards off.

When they got out on land, they saw a charcoal fire in place, with fish laid out on it, and bread. Jesus said to them, "Bring some of the fish that you have just caught." So Simon Peter went aboard and hauled the net ashore, full of large fish, 153 of them. And although there were so many, the net was not torn. Jesus said to them, "Come and have breakfast." Now none of the disciples dared ask him, "Who are you?" They knew it was the Lord. Jesus came and took the bread and gave it to them, and so with the fish. This was now the third time that Jesus was revealed to the disciples after he was raised from the dead.

John 21:1-14

When they had finished breakfast, Jesus said to Simon Peter, "Simon, son of John, do you love me more than these?" He said to him, "Yes, Lord; you know that I love you." He said to him, "Feed my lambs." He said to him a second time, "Simon, son of John, do you love me?" He said to him, "Yes, Lord; you know that I love you." He said to him, "Tend my sheep." He said to him the third time, "Simon, son of John, do you love me?" Peter was grieved because he said to him the third time, "Do you love me?" and he said to him, "Lord, you know everything; you know that I love you." Jesus said to him, "Feed my sheep.

Truly, truly, I say to you,
when you were young, you used to dress yourself
and walk wherever you wanted,
but when you are old, you will stretch out your hands,
and another will dress you and carry you where you do not want to go."

(This he said to show by what kind of death he was to glorify God.) And after saying this he said to him, "Follow me."

Peter turned and saw the disciple whom Jesus loved following them, the one who had been reclining at table close to him and had said, "Lord, who is it that is going to betray you?" When Peter saw him, he said to Jesus, "Lord, what about this man?" Jesus said to him, "If it is my will that he remain until I come, what is that to you? You follow me!" So the saying spread abroad among the brothers that this disciple was not to die; yet Jesus did not say to him that he was not to die, but, "If it is my will that he remain until I come, what is that to you?" This is the disciple who is bearing witness about these things, and who has written these things, and we know that his testimony is true.

Now there are also many other things that Jesus did.

Were every one of them to be written,

I suppose that the world itself

could not contain the books that would be written.

(A 'floating' story of an incident not recorded
in the earliest manuscripts of John)

They went each to his own house, but Jesus went to the Mount of Olives.

Early in the morning he came again to the temple. All the people came to him, and he sat down and taught them. The scribes and the Pharisees brought a woman who had been caught in adultery, and placing her in the midst they said to him, "Teacher, this woman has been caught in the act of adultery. Now in the Law Moses commanded us to stone such women. So what do you say?" This they said to test him, that they might have some charge to bring against him.

Jesus bent down and wrote with his finger on the ground. And as they continued to ask him, he stood up and said to them,

"Let him who is without sin among you
be the first to throw a stone at her."

And once more he bent down and wrote on the ground.

But when they heard it, they went away one by one, beginning with the older ones, and Jesus was left alone with the woman standing before him. Jesus stood up and said to her, "Woman, where are they? Has no one condemned you?" She said, "No one, Lord." And Jesus said, "Neither do I condemn you; go, and from now on sin no more."

John 7:53-8:11

Artist's Postscript

Flinders Ranges
Nuthawinji
Broken Hill
Darling River
Menindee (Kinchega)
Mungo
Mildura
Newcastle
Canberra
Murray River

Postscript: a few Artist's comments

'Stories are the secret reservoir of values: change the stories individuals or nations live by and tell themselves, and you change the individuals or nations' says Nobel Laureate Ben Okri, quoted by Wheye and Kennedy (2008:73).

John tells a story of love and hope, recording the cosmic reality that God, the Creator and Governor of the universe, becomes human to reconcile an alienated humanity to himself!

We in the West have become so blasé – or so dismissive – of an idea that two millennia ago was so earth-shatteringly radical that even the experts in the Jewish Scriptures (the clearest communication of God with humanity) were unprepared and incredulous.

But in fact God had been preparing them for centuries, showing them what it would take to be reconciled, through layers of symbols foreshadowing Jesus' coming: the sacrificed lamb; the scapegoat; the ladder accessing heaven and earth; the serpent lifted up; the manna from heaven… They were there to show that the only way of being reconciled *had* to come from God; and that all wrong – from the Garden of Eden in Genesis 2 onwards – really came down to lack of trust in him.

However, even without these layers, outsiders like ourselves can still understand John's images of light and life, water and bread that God provides, which symbolise his sustaining us in his new Creation offered through his Son.

The other revolutionary concept in *John* is that 'the Lord who is one' is so because the 3 persons of God – the Father, the Son and the Spirit – are

so united, *so* of one mind and heart that they act in one accord. And that, understandably, deeply offended the Jewish leaders of the day. But it is essential for reconciliation. God takes flesh and blood, so that Jesus, as Son of God, represents God in a way that speaks to all our senses. And as Son of Man, he faultlessly represents humanity to God. He *is* the ladder that bridges earth and heaven. He *himself* is the way to the Father and thus to eternal life, both the *means* (through his death and rising) and the *decider* (as judge of all). He dies as the representative Passover lamb, in order to be resurrected , creating a pathway to God. In his coming and returning to the Father via the Cross, he judges the 'ruler of this world' (Satan) and frees us from his hold over us, which binds us to death and unfulfilment. Knowing what it is like to be human – to be weary and to weep – he can sympathise with our weaknesses.

The Son's becoming flesh is not magic or fairy tale. And neither are the *signs* he does. Responsible for the formation of the universe, its provision and restoration, Jesus' capacity to perform them are as natural to him as breathing is to us.

I chose *John* because I saw it as the 'Gospel of Festivals' – a fitting sequel to *The Scrolls Illuminated*, the book of Jewish Festival Scrolls, which I published in 2011. It also works thematically: *The Song* celebrates love 'stronger than death' in a garden; *Ruth* celebrates life given through a 'Restorer of life' following a visit from the Lord; *Lamentations* and *John* are both written under the shadow of Jerusalem sacked and the nation of Israel dispersed (587BC and 70 AD); and *Esther* in the context of superpower oppression. *Ecclesiastes* writes in 3:11, 'He has put eternity into man's heart…' and Peter says to Jesus in *John* 6:68, 'To whom shall we go? You have the words of eternal life'.

In 2011 and 2012 rain fell in a way not experienced for decades in the semi-arid regions of outback New South Wales. Water flowed in the permanent river systems and filled the ephemeral lakes. Dry watercourses overflowed and as quickly emptied, leaving deep oxide-red banks and heaps of stones. The red ochre of the vast flat landscape was overlaid with random patterns of pale grey-green varieties of saltbush and hopbush, and the bright olive greens of mintbushes, acacias and eucalypts —mallees and mulgas and wilgas – like a huge Fred Williams' canvas.

When I saw it in the winter of 2012, bird life flourished in and around the waters, and the surrounding country abounded with life. I saw families of emus, kangaroos and wallabies, sheep and wild goats, shingle-back lizards and echidnas – and dingos and foxes. They all abide and abound due to the renewing water.

My field trip to capture this experience in sketches and photographs was inspiring. I felt that the landscape could convey all the images of the light and life that water brings and the Gospel celebrates.

The final book illustrations are not intended to resemble the country in which the Gospel is set, nor retell the Gospel story, nor be a comprehensive picture of the outback. But, although I have taken some artistic license, they are a faithful portrayal of the landscape I joyfully discovered.

I didn't ever see the red-tailed black cockatoo out west, though it is in its National Parks' fauna lists. To me it represents the Lord – in its graceful and majestic flight movement, its outspread wings cruciform; its colours of black and red (and yellow in the female) symbolising death and glory. I drew them in the local reserve's aviary, and its feather given by a friend. A second brief trip to the Flinders inspired the illustrations on pages 13, 33 and 67.

I have set out *John's* text for you to enter into yourself. However, it is based on my careful research into *John* and a wide range of theological discussion on it. If you would like to know more about my decision-making journey, you can contact me via my website fionapfennigwerth.info.

References
Outline of Australia sketched from *The Macquarie World Atlas* (Macquarie Library) 1984 p153
Wheye, Darryl and Donald Kennedy 2008 *Humans, Nature, and Birds: Science art from cave walls to computer screens* New Haven London: Yale University Press

And a few thankyous

To my husband Ross and friend Ruth Colman for their loving and editorial support

To Charles Sturt University, particularly my Masters in Theology supervisors Peter Pocock and Gerard Moore

To Rachael Ainsworth for her expert help in InDesign

To Virginia Wheeler, for her trustworthy car for my outback journey

To tour operators Tri-State Tours for the Mutawintji and Kinchega excursions; Harry Nanya tour to Mungo; and Derek Schneidereit for his b&b and Flinders tour

To Bruce Ramsay for his permission to use his photograph of a fairy martin

To my sister Felicity Tipper for her photographs of emus and red-capped robin in the Flinders

To my Bible study groups, who encountered *John* over long periods

And to a host of friends and family for their encouragement

Fiona Pfennigwerth

National Library of Australia Cataloguing-in-Publication Data

The Gospel according to John Illuminated

ISBN 978-0-646-91246-2
Religion and Theology

With my grateful thanks,

Email: fiona@fionapfennigwerth.info

Printed in Singapore by Tien Wah Press (Pte) Ltd
Technical InDesign expertise: Rachael Ainsworth - 0431 585 402
Distributed by The Bible Society in Australia

*With thanks to Andrew and Barbara Podger & Margo Sietsma
whose generosity realised this book's publication!*